DIRECTIVES & RULINGS ON FINISHING THE MONTH OF RAMADHAN

SHAYKH ABDUR RAZZAAQ BIN ABDUL MUHSIN AL-BADR

ISBN: 978-1-9432-8094-0

First Edition: Ramadhaan 1436 A.H./July 2015 C.E.

Cover Design by Maktabatulirshad staff

Translation by Hakim Ihsan Muwwakkil
Revision by Maktabatulirshad staff

Editing by Maktabatulirshad staff

Typesetting & Formatting by Aboo Sulaymaan Muhammad AbdulAzim bin Joshua Baker

Printing: Ohio Printing

Subject: Admonition

Website: www.maktabatulirshad.com
E-mail: info@maktabatulirshad.com

Contents

INTRODUCTION

BRIEF BIOGRAPHY OF THE AUTHOR

His name: Shaykh 'Abdur-Razzaaq Bin 'Abdul-Muhsin Al-'Abbad Al-Badr.

He is the son of Al-'Allamah Muhaddith of Medina Shaykh 'Abdul-Muhsin Al-'Abbad Al-Badr.

Birth: He was born on the 22nd day of Dhul-Qaddah in the year 1382 AH in az-Zal fi, Kingdom of Saudi Arabia. He currently resides in Al-Medina Al-Munawwarah.

Current Occupation: He is a member of the teaching staff at the Islamic University, in Al-Medina.

Scholastic certifications: Doctorate in Aqeedah.

The Shaykh has authored books, researches, as well as numerous explanations in different sciences. Among them:

1. Fiqh of Supplications & Ad-Dhkaar.

[4]

2. Hajj & refinement of Souls,

3. Explanation of the book "Exemplary Principles" By Shaykh Uthaymeen (May Allāh have mercy upon him).

4. Explanation of the book "the principles of Names & Attributes" authored by Shaykh-ul-Islam Ibn-Qayyim (May Allāh have mercy upon him).

5. Explanation of the book "Good Words" authored by Shaykh-ul-Islam Ibn Qayyim (May Allāh have mercy upon him).

6. Explanation of the book "Aqeedah Tahaawiyyah".

7. Explanation of the book "Fusuul: Biography of the Messenger) By Ibn Katheer (May Allāh have mercy upon him).

8. He has a full explanation of the book "Aadaab-ul-Muf'rad" authored by Imam Bukhari (May Allāh have mercy upon him).

From the most distinguished scholars whom he has taken knowledge and acquired knowledge from are:

1. His father Al-'Allamah Shaykh 'Abdul-Muhsin Al-Badr — may Allāh preserve him.

2. Al-'Allamah Shaykh Ibn Baaz—may Allāh have mercy upon him.

3. Al-'Allamah Shaykh Muhammad Bin Saleh Al-'Uthaymeen—may Allāh have mercy upon him.

4. Shaykh Ali Nasir Faqeehi—may Allāh preserve him.

ARABIC SYMBOL TABLE

Arabic Symbols & their meanings

رَضِيَ ٱللَّهُ عَنْهُ	May Allaah be pleased with him (i.e. a male companion of the Prophet Muhammad)
سُبْحَانَهُ وَتَعَالَى	Glorified & Exalted is Allaah
عَزَّوَجَلَّ	(Allaah) the Mighty & Sublime
تَبَارَكَ وَتَعَالَى	(Allaah) the Blessed & Exalted
جَلَّ وَعَلَا	(Allaah) the Sublime & Exalted
عَلَيْهِ ٱلصَّلَاةُ وَٱلسَّلَامُ	May Allaah send Blessings & Safety upon him (i.e. a Prophet or Messenger)
صَلَّى ٱللَّهُ عَلَيْهِ وَعَلَى آلِهِ وَسَلَّمَ	May Allaah send Blessings & Safety upon him and his family (i.e. Du'aa send mentioned the Prophet Muhammad)
رَحِمَهُ ٱللَّهُ	May Allaah have mercy upon him
رَضِيَ ٱللَّهُ عَنْهُمْ	May Allaah be pleased with them (i.e. Du'aa made for the Companions of the Prophet Muhammad)
جَلَّ جَلَالُهُ	(Allaah) His Majesty is Exalted
رَضِيَ ٱللَّهُ عَنْهَا	May Allaah be pleased with her (i.e. a female companion of the Prophet Muhammad)

INTRODUCTION

All praise is due to Allāh, the Lord of all the Worlds. I bear witness that there is no deity worthy of Worship except Allāh, He is Alone without any partners and I bear witness that Muhammad is His Slave and Messenger and may the blessings and peace of Allāh be upon him and his family and his companions altogether. As for that which follows;

O, my noble brothers! We are now living the last moments of this great season and the Blessed Month of Ramadhan, and the days of this blessed month have passed that were occupied with fasting and prayer and the remembrance of Ar-Rahmaan[1] Sublime is He and Most High. And spent the following nights of it occupied with prayer, invoking, seeking refuge, and mentioning Allāh High in His Majesty. Allāh, He is Al-Manaan[2], Al-Mutafadhal[3], High is He in His Majesty

---

[1] This is one of the Names of Allah which is translated meaning The Most Gracious and is only for Allah. Derived from the name is the attribute of His Mercy which He gives to all of His creation.
[2] This name of Allah which means the One Who bestows blessings or the Benefactor.
[3] This name of Allah which means the One Who give and bestows virtues or favors.

and Al-Muyassir[4], Al-Mu'een[5], Al-Haadi to the straight path.

There is no doubt that the arriving of this great season and reaching this virtuous time and the aiding of it upon obedience to Allāh, from prayer, fasting, remembrance (of Allāh), recitation of Allāh's Speech (Al-Quraan), giving charity, spending in the cause of Allāh, kindness to the parents, and other than these different types of righteousness, all of this which is from the great favors and bountiful blessings that necessitates thanks to The Bestower of Blessings (سُبْحَانَهُوَتَعَالَى). So contemplate deeply of this occasion, May Allāh protect you, and that which Allāh (سُبْحَانَهُوَتَعَالَى) has completed with the verse of the fasting mentioned in Surah Al-Baqarah beginning with His statement:

﴿ شَهْرُ رَمَضَانَ ٱلَّذِىٓ أُنزِلَ فِيهِ ٱلْقُرْءَانُ ﴾

"The Month of Ramadhan, which in it the Quraan was sent down."

Contemplate deeply Allāh (سُبْحَانَهُوَتَعَالَى) completed it with His statement:

---

[4] This name of Allah which means the One Who makes things easy.

[5] This name of Allah which means The Helper.

INTRODUCTION

$$\text{﴿ وَلَعَلَّكُمْ تَشْكُرُونَ ۝ ﴾}$$

"So perhaps you may be thankful." [*Soorah al-Baqarah* 2:185]

After He High is He in His Majesty, mentioned the numerous blessings and bountiful benefits and different gifts which necessitate thanks to the Bestower of Blessings Sublime. Allāh Glory to Him says:

$$\text{﴿ شَهْرُ رَمَضَانَ ٱلَّذِىٓ أُنزِلَ فِيهِ ٱلْقُرْءَانُ هُدًى لِّلنَّاسِ وَبَيِّنَٰتٍ مِّنَ ٱلْهُدَىٰ وَٱلْفُرْقَانِ فَمَن شَهِدَ مِنكُمُ ٱلشَّهْرَ فَلْيَصُمْهُ وَمَن كَانَ مَرِيضًا أَوْ عَلَىٰ سَفَرٍ فَعِدَّةٌ مِّنْ أَيَّامٍ أُخَرَ يُرِيدُ ٱللَّهُ بِكُمُ ٱلْيُسْرَ وَلَا يُرِيدُ بِكُمُ ٱلْعُسْرَ وَلِتُكْمِلُوا۟ ٱلْعِدَّةَ وَلِتُكَبِّرُوا۟ ٱللَّهَ عَلَىٰ مَا هَدَىٰكُمْ وَلَعَلَّكُمْ تَشْكُرُونَ ۝ ﴾}$$

"The Month of Ramadhan, which in it the Quraan was sent down as a guidance for mankind and clear proofs for the guidance and criterion. So whoever of you sights the crescent (on the first night of) the month, then he must

[10]

observe fasting it. **Whoever was ill or on a journey, then the same amount of days (he did not observe fasting) can make up from other days. Allāh wants ease for you and not want difficulty for you, and that you complete the same number (of days) and that you must recognize His Greatness for that which He has guided you and that perhaps you may be thankful."** [*Soorah al-Baqarah* 2:185]

How many of these blessings have been mentioned and benefits were enumerated in this Noble Verse?!

The blessing of this great month was mentioned with its goodness and its blessings and the bestowed favors of Allāh (سُبْحَانَهُوَتَعَالَى) to His servants in it, and it is the best of the months and the absolutely most virtuous of them and the exalted of them and the greatest of them.

And in this month, there is the greatest of blessings, and a tremendous gift which it is revelation of the Quraan;

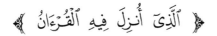

"Which in it the Quraan was sent down."

This is clearly a tremendous blessing. The Quraan which is a guidance to mankind and clear proofs from

[11]

the guidance and criterion. The Quraan which guides to that which is best. The Quraan which in it is happiness for the servants and success for them in this life and the Hereafter. Also, the revelation of the Quraan was in a night from the nights of this month that it was revealed which is the Night of Decree. Allāh has made this night very honorable, extremely important, and highly ranked. And made this night from its virtues and great blessings that it is better than one thousand months, meaning that it is better than about eighty- three years. There is no doubt that this proves this night is honored, very important, is a great occasion, and the goodness and blessings are increased in it.

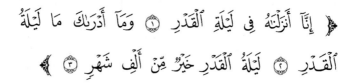

"Verily, We have sent it (Al-Quraan) in the Night of Decree. And what will make you know the Night of Decree. The Night of Decree is better than one thousand months." [*Soorah al-Qadr* 97: 1 -3]

From these favors, the blessing of observing this month and being blessed with observing its fasting;

"So whoever of you sights the crescent (on the first night of) the month, then he must observe fasting it."

There is no doubt that if you observed this month, Oh believer, observing this month of fasting, granted with good health, well-being, and peace while observing this obedience and carrying out this act of worship, then it is clear that this is a great favor that Allāh Blessed is He The Most High made easy for you and bestowed upon you. So how many people observed fasting with us last Ramadhan, and how many of them observed fasting with us in the beginning of this month and did not finish its days and they did not reach this year, but they were with us last year or the years before it? So for you reaching this month and observing it and observing fasting was made easy for you and obedience and worship, then this is from the great blessings and apparent favors bestowed upon you that Allāh Blessed is He The Most High made easy for you.

From these favors which were mentioned in this verse, the easiness of Allāh Glory to Him and that our religion makes it easy upon the one who is sick or on a journey, which fasting can be difficult for him;

[13]

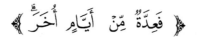

﴿ فَعِدَّةٌ مِّنْ أَيَّامٍ أُخَرَ ﴾

"Then the same amount of days (he did not observe fasting) can make up from other days."

He can observe fasting in place of those days some other days after Ramadhan.

From the Favors of Allāh (سُبْحَانَهُوَتَعَالَى) upon us which is mentioned in this verse, His statement:

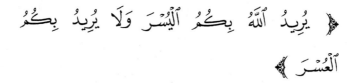

﴿ يُرِيدُ ٱللَّهُ بِكُمُ ٱلْيُسْرَ وَلَا يُرِيدُ بِكُمُ ٱلْعُسْرَ ﴾

"Allāh wants ease for you and not want difficulty for you."

This is not specifically for fasting alone; rather it is in all of the affairs of the religion altogether because our entire religion is easy like the Prophet (صَلَّىٱللَّهُعَلَيْهِوَسَلَّمَ) said:

إِنَّ الدِّينَ يُسْرٌ ، وَ لَنْ يُشَادَّ الدِّينَ أَحَدٌ إِلَّا غَلَبَهُ ، فَسَدِّدُوا وَ قَارِبُوا وَ أَبْشِرُوا

"Indeed the religion is very easy, and whoever overburdens himself in his religion will not be able to continue in that way. So you should not

**be extremists, but try to be near to perfection
and receive the good tidings that you will be
rewarded."[6]**

From the great favors of Allāh (سُبْحَانَهُوَتَعَالَى) that is
mentioned in this verse, to complete the days, the
amount of days of not observing the fast. This is a
blessing that Allāh blessed you to observe this month
and observe fasting completely up until the last day of
the month. And to completing of the month is on
sunset night of the 'Eid[7] and with that those days of
fasting were completed and this easy righteousness
and these blessings of Allāh (سُبْحَانَهُوَتَعَالَى) bestowed and
prepared for His Servants.

Also from those favors, that which is legislated for you
in completing these days of fasting to Say *"Allāhu
Akbar,"* Allāh is the Greatest (*Takbeer*), Exalting Him,
(سُبْحَانَهُوَتَعَالَى)

$$﴿ \text{وَلِتُكْمِلُواْ الْعِدَّةَ وَلِتُكَبِّرُواْ اللَّهَ عَلَى مَا هَدَىٰكُمْ} ﴾$$

---

[6] Reported by Al-Bukhari (39) Narrated by Abu Hurayrah (May
Allah be pleased with him)
[7] 'Eid which is translated meaning feast or holiday which in
Islam there are two

"That you must Exalt Him in His Greatness for that which He has guided you."

The *Takbeer* starts at sunset on the night of the Feast, with the calling of Maghrib prayer when the sun has set and this ends the month of observing the fast and the month of Shawwal begins and the first days of the Feast of Al-Fitr (Breaking Fast of Ramadhan). And this is a great and blessed day, which this is a hint to that which come of mentioning some of the rules and regulations concerning it. These great favors and lofty blessings were enumerated and mentioned in this Noble Verse then was concluded with His Statement:

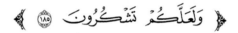

"So that perhaps you may be thankful."

So it is upon us, Oh assembly of believers, assembly of fasters, to be thankful to Our Lord, and to remember His blessings, and we be confessing and admitting to His virtues, His gifts, and His bestowed blessings, and to give all our praise to Allāh Blessed is He The most High.

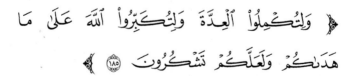

[16]

"And that you complete the same number (of days) and that you must recognize His Greatness for that which He has guided you and that perhaps you may be thankful."

We ask Allāh to grant us all with thanks of His favors and confession of His bestowed blessings and admitting to His benefits, His preferences, His gifts and to make us from those of His thankful remembering servants and that He protects us altogether from the evils of ourselves and evil deeds, and to accept us from us (our good deeds) in best manner, and forgive us for our mistakes, or forgetting, or negligence, or shortcomings, as we are those of short-comings.

كُلُّ بَنِي آدَمَ خَطَّاءٌ وَ خَيْرُ الْخَطَّائِينَ التَّوَّابُونَ

"All of the children of Adam make mistakes, but the best of them are those who repent."[8]

---

[8] Reported by Ibn Majah (4251) Narrated by Anas (May Allah be pleased with him). This Hadith was declared to be a Fair Hadith by Ash-Shaykh Al-Albani in his book As-Sahih Al-Jami' As-Sagheer (4515) (May Allah have mercy upon him).

INTRODUCTION

We ask Allāh, the Sublime and Most High to end our month with forgiveness and pleasure, rescue from the Hell-Fire, with success to obedience to The Most Gracious (سُبْحَانَهُ وَتَعَالَى).

O Assembly of my Noble brothers, indeed from the best things to be cautious of similar to this time, that we remember very well that these acts of worship, and different types of obedience that are made easy in the Month of Ramadhan and have been set in place in this blessed season, so it is not becoming that our last time doing these acts of obedience, like fasting, or praying at night, or reciting Quraan, or giving charity, or spending wealth or other than these types of righteousness and obedience that Allāh made easy for us in this great month, rather it should be that the month of Ramadhan is the opening the doors of goodness, and a noble entrance of engaging upon doing acts of obedience. It should not be that the person after finishing this month that he cuts off from obedience and leaves these acts of worship. And because there are some people, if Ramadhan finishes, they become lazy in worship, even those who leave off that which is compulsory and obligations of the religion!! And this is worst it could be and most harmful for that person.

From that which has been mentioned by the People of Knowledge that from the signs of the acceptance (of Allāh) of fasting and night praying, and the different types of worship that were made easy in the month of Ramadhan that the person's condition becomes better after Ramadhan because good deeds calls on his siblings. So from the signs of acceptance is that the condition of the person after Ramadhan is a pleasant condition, by preserving that which compulsory and obligations of the religion and is far from prohibitions and sins. That is from the signs and evidences of acceptance.

On the other hand, may Allāh protect, if the person finds within himself after Ramadhan engaging in disobedience and searching for sins and became far from obedience and compulsory acts of worship, then this is not evidence of good and not from the signs of acceptance. Verily the Prophet (صَلَّى ٱللَّٰهُ عَلَيْهِ وَسَلَّمَ) said:

رَغِمَ أَنْفُ رَجُلٍ دَخَلَ عَلَيْهِ رَمَضَانُ ثُمَّ انْسَلَخَ
قَبْلَ أَنْ يُغْفَرَ لَهُ

[19]

INTRODUCTION

"Reluctant is the man that enter upon him Ramadhan then it ended before he was forgiven (by Allāh)."[9]

If this was the condition of the person after Ramadhan changes, an embarrassing condition, the condition of negligence in the compulsories of Islam, and obligations of the religion and in it neglection and laziness especially with the mandatory prayer and engaging in evil deeds and prohibitions, then this is not from the good signs and not from the signs of acceptance. So because of this, the best advice is for the servant to strive after Ramadhan to be upright upon obedience and to remember that the Lord of Ramadhan, He is the Lord of Shawwal, and the Lord of Shawwal, He is the Lord of all the month of the year, and that worship is expected from the servant his entire lifespan

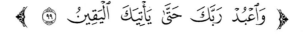

﴿ وَٱعۡبُدۡ رَبَّكَ حَتَّىٰ يَأۡتِيَكَ ٱلۡيَقِينُ ۝ ﴾

---

[10] Reported by At-Tirmidhi (3545) Narrated by Abu Hurayrah (May Allah be pleased with him). This Hadith was declared to be authentic by Ash-Shaykh Al-Albani in his book As-Sahih Al-Jami' As-Sagheer (3510) (May Allah have mercy upon him)

"And worship your Lord until death falls upon you." [*Soorah al-Hijr* 15:99]

"Oh, you who have believed fear Allāh as He is worthy of being fear and do not die except in the state of Muslims." [*Soorah Aali Imran* 3:102]

Meaning that you should preserve being upon Islam the time of your good health, your well-being, and your times of ease because indeed The All Noble (سُبْحَانَهُوَتَعَالَى), made from His custom and His blessings that He would make firm the one who preserves Islam and will help him upon a pleasant ending and will die upon that and will be resurrected upon. So these matters are important and are connected, and it is a must to have special care of them. Worshipping of Allāh (سُبْحَانَهُوَتَعَالَى), is not only in a certain month or a certain time, rather this worshipping is always continuous until death falls upon the servant

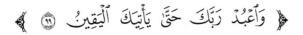

[21]

INTRODUCTION

**"And worship your Lord until there come to
you the certainty."**

Meaning until Allāh causes death to fall upon you.
The word 'certainty' refers to death. And Allāh
(سُبْحَانَهُ وَتَعَالَى) says:

﴿ إِنَّ ٱلَّذِينَ قَالُوا۟ رَبُّنَا ٱللَّهُ ثُمَّ ٱسْتَقَٰمُوا۟ تَتَنَزَّلُ
عَلَيْهِمُ ٱلْمَلَٰٓئِكَةُ أَلَّا تَخَافُوا۟ وَلَا تَحْزَنُوا۟ وَأَبْشِرُوا۟
بِٱلْجَنَّةِ ٱلَّتِي كُنتُمْ تُوعَدُونَ ۝ ﴾

**"Verily those who said our Lord is Allāh and
then stand firm the angels will descend upon
them (saying): Fear not, nor will you grieve but
receive the Glad tidings of the Paradise for that
which you have been promised."** [*Soorah Fussilat*
41:30]

And Allāh High is He in His Majesty says:

﴿ إِنَّ ٱلَّذِينَ قَالُوا۟ رَبُّنَا ٱللَّهُ ثُمَّ ٱسْتَقَٰمُوا۟ فَلَا خَوْفٌ
عَلَيْهِمْ وَلَا هُمْ يَحْزَنُونَ ۝ ﴾

[22]

**"Verily those who said Our Lord is Allāh and
then stand firm then there is no fear upon them
nor will they grieve."** [*Soorah Al-Ahqaf* 46:13]

So the servant that Allāh made it easy for him to reach
this month and helped him in it upon fasting and
praying at night and with obedience to Allāh (سُبْحَانَهُوَتَعَالَى)
and made this month the beginning of him engaging
in Allāh's obedience after Ramadhan. As for the one
who is cut off from obedience and leaves off worship
after Ramadhan, then this is a disaster and a great
misfortune. It was mentioned to one of the Righteous
Predecessor about some people that we busy with
worship in Ramadhan then if Ramadhan ended, they
became neglecting, lazy and fell behind greatly!! He
said: "Oh what evilest of people that they know Allāh
only in the month of Ramadhan." So this is a disaster
if the person does not know Allāh at a certain time of
the year, rather it is a certain month, or a certain week,
or a certain day or what is similar to that. It is
obligatory to know Allāh all the time and establishing
His worship continuously, preserving the
compulsories of Islam and carrying out that which is
obliged, stay far away from that which is forbidden
and prohibitions, but to compete in goodness and
desired and highly recommended acts of worship.
Then Our Lord Sublime and High is He in His Majesty

[23]

will show us the good within ourselves so that we may strive harder in righteous deeds and obedience to Allāh (سُبْحَانَهُوَتَعَالَى) and that we may seek help from Our Lord Sublime and High is He in His Majesty. Each one of us he will busy himself after Ramadhan in the state of doing righteous deeds and obedience and that he makes for himself a nice schedule and leave that condition that he was upon before Ramadhan, from reluctance or neglecting or similar to this. With that then he has truly benefitted from observing the fast, certainly fearing Allāh (سُبْحَانَهُوَتَعَالَى). Not everyone that fasts receive the reward for fasting that month, and everyone that stood to pray at night receives the reward for standing, instead like it was said by the Prophet (صَلَّاللَّهُعَلَيْهِوَسَلَّم) said:

رُبَّ صَائِمٍ حَظُّهُ مِنْ صِيَامِهِ الْجُوعُ وَالْعَطَشُ ، وَ رُبَّ قَائِمٍ حَظُّهُ مِنْ قِيَامِهِ السَّهَرُ .

"Perhaps the faster his reward from fasting will be only hunger and thirst or perhaps the one who stood to pray his reward for standing is only staying up late." [10]

---

[10] Reported by Al-Haakim (1571) Narrated by Abu Hurayrah (May Allah be pleased with him). This Hadith was declared to be

We ask Allāh to not prevent us all from His virtues and His bestowed favors and that he accepts our fast and accept our night prayer and to forgive for our short-comings.

As for the servant that Allāh (سُبْحَانَهُوَتَعَالَى) made this goodness easy for him and bestowed this blessing upon him then it incompetent for him to engage in obedience to Allāh (سُبْحَانَهُوَتَعَالَى) after Ramadhan. So because of this I say:

After Ramadhan is a life for striving of the person. The person is between one of two situations; Either the person that benefitted from Ramadhan and it lessons and contemplations and great sermons so this person he takes on the struggle of himself striving in obedience and ties himself to the reins of goodness that he benefitted from in the month of Ramadhan, so you find that he made a schedule for himself for reading Quraan and contemplating upon its Verses and takes out a portion of the night for praying, and he makes for himself a portion of days which he observes voluntary fasting.

authentic by Ash-Shaykh Al-Albani in his book Sahih At-Targheeb (1076) (May Allah have mercy upon him).

INTRODUCTION

مَنْ صَامَ رَمَضَانَ وَ أَتْبَعَهُ سِتًّا مِنْ شَوَّالٍ فَكَأَنَّمَا صَامَ الدَّهْرَ كُلَّهُ .

"Whoever observed fasting Ramadhan then followed it by fasting six days from Shawwal then it is as if he fasted the entire year." [11]

And the Prophet (ﷺ) said:

صَوْمُ شَهْرِ الصَّبْرِ وَ صَوْمُ ثَلَاثَةِ أَيَّامٍ مِنْ كُلِّ شَهْرٍ صَوْمُ الدَّهْرِ .

"Fasting the month of patience and Fasting three days of every month is like fasting the entire year." [12]

So after Ramadhan ends, he sets in his mind that he will fast six days of the month of Shawwal, which does not necessitate that he fast them right after the Feast, six days in a roll, but even if he spread them out and fasted them until the end of the month of Shawwal, then he is worthy of receiving this greatly blessed

[11] Reported by Muslim (1164) Narrated by Abu Ayub Al-Ansari (May Allah be pleased with him)
[12] Reported by An-Nasaaiee (2408) Narrated by Abu Hurayrah (May Allah be pleased with him). This Hadith was declared to be authentic by Ash-Shaykh Al-Albani in his book Sahih An-Nasaaiee (2408) (May Allah have mercy upon him)

reward. And also he sets his mind on Fasting three days of every month, which a good deed is rewarded ten of the likes, if you fasted three days of every month, it would be as if you observed fasting that entire month, and if you would observe fasting three days of these months, then this is fasting the entire year as mentioned in the Hadith of the Messenger (May the prayer, blessings, and peace of Allāh be upon him). Also, he sets in his mind about the prayers and spending in the cause of Allāh and many acts of righteous deeds and then strives hard at carrying them out. Allāh blessed is He, and Most High says:

$$﴿ وَٱلَّذِينَ جَٰهَدُوا فِينَا لَنَهْدِيَنَّهُمْ سُبُلَنَا وَإِنَّ ٱللَّهَ لَمَعَ ٱلْمُحْسِنِينَ ۝ ﴾$$

"And those who strive in our cause surely will be guided to Our Path and verily Allāh is with the good doers." [*Soorah Ankabut* 29:69]

And the Prophet (صَلَّى ٱللَّهُ عَلَيْهِ وَسَلَّمَ) would begin every month with a greatly blessed supplication if he saw the crescent of the new month saying:

اللَّهُمَّ أَهِلَّهُ عَلَيْنَا بِالْأَمْنِ وَ الْإِيمَانِ

[27]

INTRODUCTION

"Oh, Allāh! Let this month with safety and faith."

And in another narration:

بِـالْـيُـمْـنِ وَ الْإِيـمَـانِ وَ الـسَّـلَامَـةِ وَالْإِسْـلَامِ رَبِّي وَ رَبُّكَ

اللهُ

"With success and faith and peace and Islam, my Lord and your Lord is Allāh." [13]

In this supplication is a great benefit and the care of this has a blessing effect on the servant's month, because of you reach and entering a new month mean you have been given new time that Allāh (سُبْحَانَهُوَتَعَالَى) has granted you with and broaden your life span, and you reached it, and it was the season of deeds. The month of Ramadhan ended and then after it the month of Shawwal began and then ended then after it another month and so on. So if Allāh granted you that you reached the beginning of another month, then ask Allāh blessed is He and The Most High, to bring in the new month with safety and faith and peace and Islam for you. And all of these things are connected: There is no safety except with faith, and there is no peace

---

[13] Reported by Tirmidhi (1228), narrated by Talhah bin Ubaidullah (May Allah be pleased with him)

[28]

except with Islam. And this is guidance from the beginning of every month to take care of faith and Islam and preserving the two so that the servant will truly be upon goodness and different types of gifts from safety, peace, a pleasant lifestyle, and success with rewards from Allāh blessed is He and The Most High on the Day of Judgment.

As for faith and Islam if they are mentioned together like they were in this Hadith, then faith is meaning beliefs which their place are in the heart, Belief in Allāh, His Angels, The Revelations, The Messenger, The Last Day, and in the Pre-Ordainment from good and evil and Islam meaning all righteous good deeds and different types of worship to become close to Allāh (سُبْحَانَهُوَتَعَالَى) and before them are the compulsories of Islam and obligation of the religion that was made clear in the Hadith of Angel Jibreel when He asked the Prophet (صَلَّىاللَّهُعَلَيْهِوَسَلَّمَ):

أَخْبِرْنِي عَنِ الْإِيمَانِ ؟ قَالَ : ((أَنْ تُؤْمِنَ بِاللهِ وَ مَلَائِكَتِهِ ، وَكُتُبِهِ ، وَ رُسُلِهِ ، وَالْيَوْمِ الْآخِرِ ، وَ تُؤْمِنَ بِالْقَدَرِ خَيْرِهِ وَ شَرِّهِ)) ، قَالَ : ((أَخْبِرْنِي

عَنِ الْإِسْلَامِ ؟ فَقَالَ : ((الْإِسْلَامُ أَنْ تَشْهَدَ أَنْ لَا إِلَـهَ

إِلَّا اللهُ وَ أَنَّ مُحَـمَّـداً رَسُـولُ اللهِ صَـلَّـى اللهُ عَـلَيْـهِ وَ

سَـلَّـمَ، وَ تُـقِـيـمَ الـصَّـلَاةَ، وَ تُـؤْتِـيَ الـزَّكَـاةَ ، وَ تَـصُـومَ

رَمَـضَـانَ ، وَ تَـحُجَّ الْبَـيْـتَ إِنِ اسْـتَـطَعْـتَ إِلَيْـهِ سَبِـيلًا

.((

**"Inform me of Al-Iman (Faith)? He said: "To
believe in Allāh, His Angels, His Revelation,
His Messenger, The Last Day, and to believe in
the Pre-Ordainment from good and evil."
Inform me of Islam? "To bear witness that there
is no deity worthy of worship except Allāh and
that Muhammad is the Messenger of Allāh, to
establish the prayer, to give charity, to observe
fasting the month of Ramadhan, and to make
pilgrimage to House[14] if you can do so."[15]**

So the Prophet (ﷺ) explained faith as being
beliefs of the heart and explained Islam as being
righteous deeds and actions. So if the new month
began, then you should invoke with this supplication,

---

[14] House of Allah the Ka'bah which is in Makkah Saudi Arabia
[15] Reported by Muslim (8) Narrated by 'Umar (May Allah be
pleased with him)

asking Allāh Sublime is He High in His Majesty to grant you in it the correct belief and beautiful righteous deeds and obedience to bring you closer to Allāh (سُبْحَانَهُوَتَعَالَى), and asking Allāh (سُبْحَانَهُوَتَعَالَى), to grant you the benefits and fruitful results based upon that safety and honorable lifestyle in this life and the Hereafter.

This is goodness of the religion, obedience to Allāh and preserving His commandments (سُبْحَانَهُوَتَعَالَى) is goodness for this life and the Hereafter, and if you have goodness in religious practice, then your worldly life and your life in the Hereafter will have goodness as it was made clear in previously mentioned supplication. Also it has been authentic narration from the supplications of our Prophet (صَلَّىٱللَّهُعَلَيْهِوَسَلَّمَ) reported by Muslim[16] that he said:

اللَّهُمَّ أَصْلِحْ لِي دِينِي الَّذِي هُوَ عِصْمَةُ أَمْرِي، وَ أَصْلِحْ لِي دُنْيَايَ الَّتِي فِيهَا مَعَاشِي، وَ أَصْلِحْ لِي آخِرَتِي الَّتِي فِيهَا مَعَادِي.

"Oh Allāh set me right in my religion which is a safeguard of my affairs and set right for me my worldly life which is my way of living, and

---

[16] Reported by Muslim (2720)

set right for me my life of the Hereafter which is my eternal destiny depends upon."

So goodness in this worldly life which in it is livelihood in this life and the Hereafter which in it is returning to Allāh (سُبْحَانَهُ وَتَعَالَى) will not have goodness except with goodness in religious practice and for that purpose, it comes before everything. You will greatly benefit from this if you focus on having goodness in your religious practice and before focusing on any other affairs, because goodness in your religious practice by obeying you Lord (سُبْحَانَهُ وَتَعَالَى) and believe in Him and believe in everything that He commanded you to believe in along with belief in Him (سُبْحَانَهُ وَتَعَالَى), and to establish the compulsories of Islam and the obligations of the religion. This religion is goodness for you in your worldly life and the life in the Hereafter for you and happiness for you in this worldly life and the Hereafter.

Oh, my noble brothers! From that which should be cautious of at times like this is rules and regulations that are connected to the closing of this month properly and the most importance of the topics are three:

FIRST: ZAKAT [17] AL-FITR [18]

This is a dish[19] of food, which was narrated in different Hadiths of the Messenger (صَلَّى ٱللَّهُ عَلَيْهِ وَسَلَّمَ) that it is obligatory upon the male, female, child, adult, free, and slave person from the Muslims. This is called Zakat Al-Fitr because it is connected to ending observing the fast of Ramadhan. It is obligatory for every person that was present during some part of Ramadhan, even a little. If there was a child born before sunset of the last day of Ramadhan, then it obligatory to pay Zakat upon him, because it is obligatory to pay upon every male, female, freed person, slave, child and adult. So whoever born even a few moments before sunset on the last day of Ramadhan, then it is obligatory to pay Zakat upon him. As for the one that was still in his mother's wound then it is not obligatory to pay Zakat upon him,

---

[17] Zakat which means charity, and it is charity that is given to the poor Muslims.

[18] Fitr means to stop fasting whether it is for that day or the ending of Ramadhan which what is meant here.

[19] This dish of food is equal to eight palm full of a large size man, or now in metric weight about 2.3lbs or 1 kilogram.

but it is highly recommended because of that which was narrated by some of the Companions of the Prophet (ﷺ) mentioning that but not obligatory. But the one who was born before sunset, even a few moments before then pay Zakat upon him is obligatory, and whoever was born after sunset, then it is not obliged but it is highly recommended as mentioned before.

This Zakat is for al-Fitr, connected to thanking The Great Lord and The Bestower of Blessings, The Most Generous, and a purification to the payer of charity, feeding of the poor people. It was reported by Al-Bukhari and Muslim in their Collections of Authentic Hadiths narrated by Ibn 'Umar (May Allāh be pleased with them) he said:

فَرَضَ رَسُولُ اللهِ صَـلَّى اللهُ عَـلَيْهِ وَ سَـلَّمَ زَكَاةَ الْـفِطْرِ صَاعًا مِنْ تَـمْرٍ أَوْ صَاعًا مِنْ شَعِيرٍ عَـلَى الْـعَبْدِ وَ الْـحُرِّ، وَ الـذَّكَرِ وَ الْأُنْثَى، وَ الصَّـغِيرِ وَ الْكَبِيرِ مِنَ الْمُسْلِمِينَ.

"The Messenger of Allāh (ﷺ) obliged the giving of Zakat Al-Fitr being a dish of dates, or dish of barley to be taken out upon the slave,

[34]

free person, male, female, child, and adult from the Muslims." [20]

So it is obligatory upon the head of the household, to pay take out charity for himself and everyone that he is responsible for in his household from his wife and children and he pays charity for every single one of them a dish of food. And it was reported by Al-Bukhari and Muslim narrated by Abu Sa'eed Al-Khudari (رَضِيَاللَّهُعَنْهُ) he said:

كُنَّا نُخْرِجُ فِي عَهْدِ رَسُولِ الله صَلَّى اللهُ عَلَيْهِ وَ
سَلَّمَ يَوْمَ الْفِطْرِ صَاعًا مِنْ طَعَامٍ

"We used to pay Zakat at the time during the life of the Prophet (صَلَّىَاللَّهُعَلَيْهِوَسَلَّمَ) the Day of Fitr a dish of food." [21]

So with this being said, Zakat Al-Fitr is not to be given except as food; a dish of dates, or a dish of wheat, or a dish of barley, or a dish of cottage cheese, or a dish of raisins, or a dish of rice, millets, or corn, or other than these which are considered food. Every food which more chosen to the people of that country or more beloved to them, or frequently used by them, it is more

---

[20] Reported by Al-Bukhari (1503) and Muslim (984)
[21] Reported by Al-Bukhari (1506) and Muslim (985)

suitable because it agrees with the need of the poor people that the charity will be given to them, and it agrees with their desire. But if some food was given to him that he is not used to and something he does not always eat, or he has no need for it, them that will not fulfil his need, and because of this, the person should make sure that he gives charity of the people of that country. Food that is known, and the people are used to and is liked the people, they eat constantly, and they desire it.

Paying out money instead will not be accepted. Some people pay cash for Zakat Al-Fitr, but this is not accepted because there was currency present at the time of the Prophet (ﷺ). The drachma and dinar were present yet food was commanded to be given out as charity. And the Companions (May Allāh be pleased with them) if they informed of their actions at the time of the Prophet (ﷺ) similar to that in the Hadith of Abu Sa'eed Al-Khudari (رضي الله عنه). They informed that they would pay the charity as food, and they did not give it out in money and currency was present at their time. So it is improper for the person in this type of matter, to present his opinion instead of the Hadith of The Messenger of Allāh (ﷺ). Some people insist on putting forward his opinion instead of accepting the clear evidence.[22] Currency was present during the time of the Prophet (ﷺ) and the time of his Companions after his death, and they were not commanded except to pay the charity in food.

$$ فَرَضَ رَسُولُ اللهِ صَلَّى اللهُ عَلَيْهِ وَ سَلَّمَ زَكَاةَ الْفِطْرِ صَاعًا مِنْ تَمْرٍ أَوْ صَاعًا مِنْ شَعِيرٍ . $$

"The Messenger of Allāh (ﷺ) obliged the giving of Zakat Al-Fitr being a dish of dates or a dish of barley..."

Abu Sa'eed said:

$$ كُنَّا نُخْرِجُ فِي عَهْدِ رَسُولِ اللهِ صَلَّى اللهُ عَلَيْهِ وَ سَلَّمَ يَوْمَ الْفِطْرِ صَاعًا مِنْ طَعَامٍ . $$

"We used to pay Zakat at the time during the life of the Prophet (ﷺ) the Day of Fitr a dish of food."

---

[22] Clear evidence is either from the Qur'anic Verses or the Authentic narration from the Sunnah of the Prophet (May the blessings and peace of Allah be upon him).

So the charity is not given out except as food and whoever paid it in money, then it is not accepted. Only food that you buy will be accepted from a dish of rice, barley, wheat, dates, or raisins or other than these items, and for every single person in your family that you give for each one of them on a dish. Even if you came some of the times with this food from the house, like a bag of rice from your home and your children and your wife are all together and you have a dish ready, then you start weighing in a dish for each family member from the bag of rice. This dish is for me, this one is for my mother, this one is for so and so and this on for so and so, also this will make the children familiar, and give them the feeling of the importance of knowing that this an act of worship, and it will be said,

"We will take this charity to some poor Muslims."

This is a purification for the fast observer and the feeding of some poor Muslims; the children also live in the homes with knowing the great feeling of this important act of worship.

It was narrated by Ibn Abbaas (May Allāh be pleased with them) that was reported by Sunan Abi Dawud and other than him, he said:

[38]

فَرَضَ رَسُولُ الله صَلَّى اللهُ عَلَيْهِ وَ سَلَّمَ زَكَاةَ الْفِطْرِ طُهْرَةً لِلصَّائِمِ مِنَ اللَّغْوِ وَ الرَّفَثِ ، وَ طُعْمَةً لِلْمَسَاكِينَ .

"The Messenger of Allāh (صَلَّى ٱللَّهُ عَلَيْهِ وَسَلَّمَ) obliged the giving of Zakat Al-Fitr, purification of the fast observer from mistakes and obscenity, and feeding of the poor Muslims."[23]

In this Hadith, there is a benefit for the person giving charity and the one receiving the charity. A benefit for the Zakat giver and the one receiving the Zakat. As for the benefit connected to the one giving Zakat, it is the purification for him of his mistakes and obscenity, meaning in his fast, because a person while observing fast, it is a must that will be neglectful in some things, not being free of shortcomings so he may make some mistakes in statements or actions or of the likes. So then this Zakat purifies that for him,

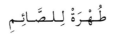

"Purification for the fast observer"

---

[23] Reported by Abu Dawud (1609)

Meaning cleanses him chastises him and purifies. Purification from what? He said:

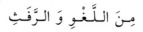

"From mistakes and obscenity."

Mistakes, meaning from mistakes in statements. And *"Ar-Rafth"* obscenity, foulness in some of the actions or statements. So it can be meant as this, foul language or actions, or it also means sexual relations and foreplay. But here in this Hadith, it does not mean sexual relations and foreplay, but what it means is obscene or foul statement or improper statements or the likes. So the Zakat Al-Fitr is a

"Purification for the fast observer"

Meaning in that which may while he is fasting from some short-comings, fault, or harm from mistakes and obscenity.

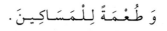

"Feeding of the poor Muslims."

When you give him food, it will be as if you are feeding him, but if you gave him clothes or you gave him

[40]

money!! In doing so, it cannot be said this is feeding because clothes are for being worn and with money maybe the poor Muslim will buy other than food. Sometimes, some poor Muslims in these days maybe fall short in the need of providing food for his children, and he does not buy food, but maybe he buys something else. I remember one of the beloved brothers who was poor and had a big family and deeply loved Islamic Books and buy them a lot even though he was poor. Sometimes, if some new books came to the bookstores, he would go to a bookstore and buy books on credit because of his appetite, passion, and desire for having books. So another beloved brother says to me: "I do not give so and so money, if I want to help him, I go to the market and buy for him rice and food and take it to his house, because if I gave him money, he would buy books." This, perhaps, is an opinion that can be taken and even if we don't know the wisdom it is obligatory upon us to obey that which has been legislated in Islam and that which has been commanded. And from the opinions that was mentioned by the People of Knowledge: Indeed it may sometimes arrive at the point of scarcity of people having food and money is available so it is preferred by the Zakat giver to pay money and to save food that he has because of the shortness of food in the country.

[41]

So the bringing the command of giving out the food to relieve the hunger of the poor Muslim and he satisfied his hunger. So because of this he said: "Feeding" and this feeding that does not happen except with food and nothing else. So giving money will not be accepted and if a person paid the *Zakat Al-Fitr* in money, then it will not be accepted and by doing so he has not given that which Allāh (سُبْحَانَهُوَتَعَالَى), has obliged him. Even if there no evidence in this matter except the statement of the Prophet (صَلَّىٰاللَّهُعَلَيْهِوَسَلَّمَ):

مَنْ عَمِلَ عَمَلاً لَيْسَ عَلَيْهِ أَمْرُنَا فَهُوَ رَدٌّ

"Whoever did an act that there is no satisfaction on our behalf then it will not be accepted."[24]

Meaning that it will not be accepted from that person, and it was not narrated in the Sunnah for paying Zakat Al-Fitr in money, but it was only narrated for paying in food.

And the time for paying the Zakat Al-Fitr is from sunset of the night of the Feast up into before the Feast Prayer. The Messenger of Allāh (صَلَّىٰاللَّهُعَلَيْهِوَسَلَّمَ) said:

أُمِرْنَا أَنْ نُؤَدِّيَهَا قَبْلَ خُرُوجِ النَّاسِ إِلَى الصَّلَاةِ

---

[24] Reported by Muslim (1718)

"We have been commanded to pay the Zakat before the people go out to the Feast Prayer."[25]

And in the Hadith of Ibn Abbaas (May Allāh be pleased with them)

فَمَنْ أَدَّاهَا قَبْلَ الـصَّلَاةِ فَهِيَ زَكَاةٌ مَـقْبُـولَةٌ، وَ مَنْ
أَدَّاهَا بَـعْدَ الـصَّلَاةِ فَـهِيَ صَـدَقَةٌ مِنَ الـصَّـدَقَاتِ .

"So whoever paid it before the prayer then it is Zakat accepted, and whoever paid it after the prayer, then is from the ordinary charities."[26]

So it is paid before the Feast Prayer. The starting time of paying it is at sunset on the night of Feast, and even if it was paid a day or two before, then it will be accepted but will not be accepted before that.

And the Zakat-ul-Fitr is to be paid in the country he is living and pay for his wife and his children and even if he authorized his wife for the country his wife is living

---

[25] Reported by Al-Bukhari (1509) and Muslim (986) narrated by 'Abdullah Bin 'Umar (May Allah be pleased with them) (May Allah be pleased with them).

[26] Reported by Abu Dawud (1609) and Ibn Majah (1827) This Hadith was declared to be a fair Hadith by Ash-Shaykh Al-Albani in his book Al-Irwa (843) May Allah have mercy upon him.

for them to pay on his behalf and theirs' then that is accepted and this affair is spacious.

Also, he pays it generously from himself and strives at finding good food, not finishing the matter by searching for any food that is present or the cheapest food to finish paying this obligation. No, but he strives at paying in that which is pleasant and search for that which is beneficial, and he is content with himself, and he presents it openhanded. Also, he's intent on looking for someone poor; some people want to free himself from paying it by any means and does not be intent on finding poor people and do not search for them. Even some of them may buy from the merchant and after he pays him say: "Do you someone that takes Zakat?" If he says yes he leaves the Zakat with the merchant and walks off!! If the merchant was not reliable or not honest maybe another person will come and he sell it to him. So it is a must that the person gives importance to the matter of Zakat and strives at paying it for himself and his family, seeking closeness to Allāh (سُبْحَانَهُوَتَعَالَى) and intending this vast goodness great benefit that is based on this Zakat.

SECOND: *TAKBEER* (SAYING "ALLĀHU AKBAR") AFTER FINISHING THE DAYS OF RAMADHAN

Surely we previously mentioned the statement of Allāh (سُبْحَانَهُوَتَعَالَى):

$$ ﴿ وَلِتُكْمِلُواْ ٱلْعِدَّةَ وَلِتُكَبِّرُواْ ٱللَّهَ عَلَىٰ مَا هَدَىٰكُمْ وَلَعَلَّكُمْ تَشْكُرُونَ ۝ ﴾ $$

"And that you complete the same number (of days) and that you must recognize His Greatness for that which He has guided you and that perhaps you may be thankful."

And this *takbeer* it is for admitting the Greatness to Allāh and Exalting Him Glory is He and High in His Majesty and showing this great legislation of Islam in openly after, completing this obligation with joy of completing this act of worship and finishing the days of observing the fasting of Ramadhan.

SECOND: TAKBEER (SAYING "ALLĀHU AKBAR") AFTER FINISHING THE DAYS OF RAMADHAN

"And that you complete the same number (of days) and that you must recognize His Greatness for that which He has guided you."

So this *takbeer* is *takbeer* for Allāh and bestowing blessings from guidance and that which He made easy and helped upon from goodness Glory to Him.

And the way to saying the *takbeer* is to say:

اللهُ أَكْـبَـرُ اللهُ أَكْـبَـرُ، لَا إِلَـهَ إِلَّا اللهُ ،وَ اللهُ أَكْـبَـرُ ، اللهُ أَكْـبَـرُ

وَ لله الْـحَـمْـدُ .

"Allāhu Akbar, Allāhu Akbar, La Ilaha Ill Allāh, Wa Allāhu Akbar, Allāhu Akbar, Wa lillahil-Hamd."

This is what has been narrated by the Noble Companions (May Allāh be pleased with them and satisfy them) and they did not increase in saying anything else like sending blessings upon the Prophet (صَلَّى ٱللَّهُ عَلَيْهِ وَسَلَّمَ) and upon his wives and his offspring or similar to that. There is no doubt that sending blessings the Prophet (صَلَّى ٱللَّهُ عَلَيْهِ وَسَلَّمَ) is from the noblest acts of worship and the best of them and exalting of them and from the greatest types of obedience. But along that, the *takbeer* was narrated from the

[46]

Companions (May Allāh be pleased with them) without mentioning this addition, and they are the more eager than us at sending blessings on the Messenger (ﷺ) and they would not add sending blessings with the *takbeer*. So it is content to do what the Companions (May Allāh be pleased with them and satisfy them) did and that which is aimed towards in the Quraan Allāh said:

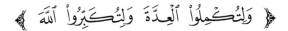

"And that you complete the same number (of days) and that you must recognize His Greatness."

So exalt Allāh (سُبْحَانَهُوَتَعَالَى) upon this description. And chanting the *takbeer* begins by completing the days of fasting as soon as the sun sets on the night of the Feast and the *takbeer* begins going to the Feast Prayer. And it is highly recommended for the Muslim to raise his voice in the Masjids, the roads, and the marketplaces announcing and raising this great legislation of Islam, *takbeer* of Allāh (سُبْحَانَهُوَتَعَالَى). And it is not legislated to make the *takbeer* altogether in a group chanting at the same time, while chanting or beginning, whether doing it with a leader or without a leader, what it meant by that is some people they have a leader that

[47]

SECOND: TAKBEER (SAYING "ALLĀHU AKBAR") AFTER FINISHING THE DAYS OF RAMADHAN

makes the *takbeer* and they say the *takbeer* along with him, or even without a leader but by starting the *takbeer* all together at once and chanting it all together until finishing, but as for making *takbeer* like this, it is not legislated because it was not narrated from the Noble Companions (May Allāh be pleased with them and satisfy them). The Eminence Ash-Shaykh 'Abdul-Aziz Bin Baz (May Allāh have mercy upon him) wrote a long, thorough report on this topic, which is also a refutation on the one which admits this type of group *takbeer* and clarified, May Allāh have mercy upon him, that this is from the acts without a foundation in the religion. Rather, this is an act of worship that every Muslim chants the *takbeer* with his own eagerness and ability and does not do along with a group while chanting and stopping the *takbeer*, but everyone chants the *takbeer* with his own ability and eagerness along his way and while he's in masjid and while he's marketplace or other than these places. He says these great numerous of *takbeer* from the time of sunset on the night of the Feast until the time of Feast Prayer, and the Feast Prayer itself has extra *takbeer*.

THIRD: RULES AND REGULATIONS DEALING WITH THE EID PRAYER

This is a greatly blessed gathering on a blessed day,
Yawm-ul Feast (Day of the Feast), the day of
happiness, the day of congratulations and joy, the day
of glad tiding, the day of breaking fast. That great day
which is the day of happiness, not wildness in it but
happiness and no arrogance in it. A feast which is
specified with the beauty of belief and the beauties of
Islam and the pure and nature of the obedience to
Allāh (سُبْحَانَهُوَتَعَالَى). A feast which its legislation is
obedience to Allāh. A feast which in it is a reunion,
fulfilling of promises, visitations, making ties with
kinfolk, and other beautiful, important matters; a feast
that is distinct from the feast of the disbelievers. The
festivals of the disbelievers celebrated with alcoholic
beverages, dancing, singing, fornication, and
misguidance, Allāh forbid that for the Community of
Islam and protect and preserve it from that. So the
Feast of the Muslims is distinct with pureness of belief
and light of faith and the glow of Islam and obedience
to Allāh (سُبْحَانَهُوَتَعَالَى) and that which truly happens
during it from unity, clinging together, and love for

[49]

one another. And this is must that the Muslim in the time of the Feast that shows Allāh (سُبْحَانَهُوَتَعَالَى) the goodness of himself from loving, purity, and reunion and leaves off separating and breaking ties, but he pardons the people and forgives and other than this from these beautiful, important matters which are necessary to be clear and apparent during the Feast.

And the Muslim, during his feast should not forget his brothers that are injured and wounded who are living in agony and pain and severe calamity by making sincere supplication for them and helping and aiding them. He does not forget his brothers, especially in Syria, which their catastrophe is great, and their afflictions are vast. Even in the month of fasting their killings, no one knows the amount of them except Allāh Glory to Him Them Most High and blood is spilled, honors are destroyed, sacred money is taken unfairly, different types of attacks going on in this great season, so the person does not forget his brothers at making sincere supplication and helping and aiding and standing beside them. And we ask Allāh Mighty is He in His Majesty to finish the Feast of the Muslims by destroying the oppressing tyrants and to relieve the servants of their evil and to bring happiness to the grief of our Muslim brothers in Syria and to quickly bring them happiness and ease and to quickly give them the greatest generosity and a pleasant, noble lifestyle filled with safety, belief, ease, joy, and happiness. And also to complete their Feast with goodness, blessing, facilitation, and comfort. Indeed, He (Allāh) blessed is He, and Most High is All-Hearing and Replies (to His servants).

So for the Feast, it is necessary to be happy or of the likes, not a feast of wildness, and not a feast for wasting money or exaggeration, and wasting and neglecting of goodness and the likes and it is not a feast for disobeying to Allāh (سُبْحَانَهُوَتَعَالَى). Some people say that the Feast is an admission for singing, sometimes some people fall into major sins and says,

"The Feast is an admission; the Feast is a time of happiness."

So he carries on in prohibited affairs and says that this is happiness of Islam, meaning that we finish Ramadhan with singing on the Feast and falling into major sin on the Feast Day!! So the Feast of the Muslims is not a time of wildness or arrogance and not a time for disobedience to Allāh (سُبْحَانَهُوَتَعَالَى), rather in it is obedience and all the likes of beauty and pleasance., and also it is a time of expressing happiness openly without disobedience to Allāh (سُبْحَانَهُوَتَعَالَى) and doing

[51]

that which Allāh High in His Majesty has prohibited upon His servants.

It is highly recommended for the Muslim to bathe, observing the Feast Prayer with a clean body, to wear fragrances, and to wear the most pleasant and best of his clothes, and should prevent have on his clothes that which is prohibited, because the origination of clothing is in that which is permissible. The legislation of Islam came with some prohibitions connected to clothing. As an example, the Prophet (ﷺ) prohibited the man from wearing silk. Also, his (the Prophet ﷺ) prohibition of wearing clothes below the ankles, as a matter of fact, there are many Hadiths about prohibiting the wearing of clothes below the ankles, even if it was just the Hadith that was reported in Sahih Muslim that the Prophet (ﷺ) said :

ثَلَاثَةٌ لَا يُكَلِّمُهُمُ اللهُ يَوْمَ الْقِيَامَةِ، وَ لَا يَنْظُرُ

إِلَيْهِمْ وَ لَا يُزَكِّيهِمْ وَ لَهُمْ عَذَابٌ أَلِيمٌ.

"Three types of people Allāh will not speak to them on the Day of Judgment nor will He look

at them nor purify them and for them is a
painful chastisement."[27]

وَ ذَكَرَ مِنْهُمْ ((الْمُسْبِلُ)) يَعْنِي الْمُسْبِلَ إِزَارَهُ .

وَ قَالَ : ((مَا أَسْفَلَ مِنَ الْكَعْبَيْنِ مِنَ الْإِزَارِ فَفِي
النَّارِ))

And then he mentioned from them the one who
lets his clothes go below his ankles, meaning
the lower garment. And also the Prophet
(صَلَّىٱللَّهُعَلَيْهِوَسَلَّمَ) said: "What is below the ankles of a
lower garment is condemned to the Hell-Fire."[28]

What would you benefit when you wear your lower
garment below your ankles, and it drags on the
ground? 'Umar Bin Al-Khattaab (رَضِيَٱللَّهُعَنْهُ) when Al-
Majoosee[29] (May Allāh curse him) stabbed him and
blood was gushing severely from his stomach and
when he drank milk, it come out of his stomach and he

---

[27] Reported by Muslim (106) This is a portion of the Hadith and
it was narrated by Abu Dharr (May Allah be pleased with him)
[28] Reported by Al-Bukhari (7563)
[29] Al-Majoos is a term in Arabic which is translated meaning a
type of pagan who worships fire, and this is their faith. They are
pagans of Persian origin. And also this title was given to the one
that killed 'Umar (May Allah be pleased with him) which he is
Abu Lulu Al-Majoosee (May Allah curse him).

was fainting, then a young boy came to him to soothe
him and said :

أَبْشِرْ يَا أَمِيرَ الْمُؤْمِنِينَ بِبُشْرَى اللهِ لَكَ ، مِنْ
صُحْبَةِ رَسُولِ اللهِ صَلَّى اللهُ عَلَيْهِ وَ سَلَّمَ، وَ قَدَمٍ
فِي الْإِسْلَا مَا قَدْ عَلِمْتَ ، ثُمَّ وَلِيتَ فَعَدَلْتَ ،
ثُمَّ شَهَادَةٌ

**"Have the glad tidings, Oh Commander of the
Believers, the glad tidings of Allāh of you being
from the amongst Companions of the
Messenger of Allāh (ﷺ) and you put
forward in Islam that which you know, then
you were put in charge of the Muslim's affairs
and being just and then you are a martyr."**

So when the young boy walked away, he said: Call that
young boy for me and said,

يَا ابْنَ أَخِي ارْفَعْ ثَوْبَكَ

"Oh son of my brother, raise your garment."

His garment was below his ankles.

[54]

ارْفَعْ ثَوْبَكَ ؛ فَإِنَّهُ أَنْقَى لِثَوْبِكَ ، وَ أَتْقَى لِرَبِّكَ

**"Raise your garment, because indeed it cleaner
of your garment and fearing of your Lord."**

Some people wear their clothes dragging on the
ground tremendously, and one of the days of this
Ramadhan, I prostrated and there was a person in front
of me. When he prostrated, his garment was covering
the place of prostration of the person behind him.
When I prostrated, when I placed my forehead, as
there were dampness and the man just came from the
lavatory (bathroom). This is what Umar said,

أَنْقَى لِثَوْبِكَ

"Cleaner for your garment."

So the point here is that the Muslim it is upon him to
fear Allāh (سُبْحَانَهُوَتَعَالَى) and it ordained that some time
passed him by and he was neglecting in this matter or
he thinks that it is not important and that it is not
necessary for him to speak about it for example, as for
that, this is his opinion but it is upon him that he has to
correct himself at being upon something and meeting
Allāh upon that and keep in his mind this Hadith:

[55]

ثَلَاثَةٌ لَا يُكَلِّمُهُمُ اللهُ يَوْمَ الْقِيَامَةِ، وَ لَا يَنْظُرُ

إِلَيْهِمْ وَ لَا يُزَكِّيهِمْ وَ لَهُمْ عَذَابٌ أَلِيمٌ.

"Three types of people Allāh will not speak to them on the Day of Judgment nor will He look at them nor purify them and for them is a painful chastisement."

I remember beautiful story: I was a while back, teaching in middle school, and there was a student in 7th or 8th grade walking in front of me and his garment was touching the ground, so I called him gently and said to him: "There is a Hadith of the Messenger of Allāh (ﷺ) I think you may not have heard it before in your life." He said: "What is the Hadith?" Then I repeated to arouse his eagerness, "I think you may not have heard it before in your life." He said: "O Professor! What is the Hadith?" I said to him: "The Prophet (ﷺ) said:

ثَلَاثَةٌ لَا يُكَلِّمُهُمُ اللهُ يَوْمَ الْقِيَامَةِ، وَ لَا يَنْظُرُ

إِلَيْهِمْ وَ لَا يُزَكِّيهِمْ وَ لَهُمْ عَذَابٌ أَلِيمٌ.

"Three types of people Allāh will not speak to them on the Day of Judgment nor will He look

**at them nor purify them and for them is a
painful chastisement."**

And he mentioned from them the one who lets his
clothes go below his ankles. Do you know what the
one who let his clothes go below the ankles means? His
lower garment is below his ankles." I said: "Have you
heard of this Hadith or not?" He said: "No, I haven't
heard this before." I said: "I am positive you have not
heard this Hadith before." Then I left him and did not
say anything else other than this. The very next day,
and as I was walking in along the way, suddenly I seen
a student running behind me, "O Professor, O
Professor!" I stopped and turned towards him, and he
said: "What do you think about this my garment?" I
said to him: "Great." I said to you that you have not
heard this Hadith. This student was in the 7th grade
and when he heard the Hadith he did not reject it, but
some adults hear this Hadith, and they reject it!! We
ask Allāh to pardon us and open our chests to good, O
Allāh! Guide our hearts to (doing) well. O Allāh!
Guide our hearts to (doing) well and give us ease in
having obedience to our Prophet (ﷺ). And the
servant should stay away from beautifying or making
pretty to himself of thinking that he should cut his
beard because there were several Hadiths narrated by
the Prophet (ﷺ) about leaving the beard and

[57]

letting it grow, and honoring it, and letting it grow. And surely the Mother of the Believers 'Ayesha (May Allāh be pleased with her) if she wanted to swear (by Allāh) she would say:

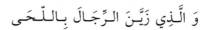

"By the One, Who beautified men giving them beards."

So the beard is the beauty of the man and his attractiveness. Some men, May Allāh guide us and them, and rectify us and rectify them and guide our hearts to good, it does not suffice that he cuts it, rather he uses different techniques to become beardless. Even to the point that of my beloved brothers, it was related by him that he says about one of the villages: "Indeed, so and so now looks like his sister." And for some of them it does not suffice to cut it, rather he uses different techniques of cosmetics from his sister to benefit from her. All of this truly is useless, neglecting, and the lack of the person knowing his reality, because the beard itself, is the beauty of man and his attractiveness and splendor of this beautiful look of him which Allāh (سُبْحَانَهُوَتَعَالَى) has honored him with.

So the point here is that indeed the person goes to the Feast with a pleasant look and also takes his wife and

[58]

his children even the menstruating women and the mature virgin staying in seclusion like that which was narrated in the Hadith of Umm 'Atiya reported by Al-Bukhari and Muslim, that they come out to observe and caught the goodness and observe the calling of the Muslims. The menstruating women do not pray, but they observe the goodness and observe the calling of the Muslims.

It is highly recommended for the Muslim to take a route when he leaves his home and when he returns, he takes a different route because of this being confirmed by the Messenger (ﷺ), and on his way to the Feast Prayer, and he does not forget the *takbeer*. He carries on making *takbeer* of Allāh (سُبْحَانَهُوَتَعَالَى) and then he attends this great prayer.

And he makes it a point to sit for the lecture, which is after the prayer. To sit and listen to the lecture is not obligatory, but is upon the person to wait and be patient so that he may listen to the sermon and conveyance that are mentioned in the lecture, and also he observes the group call that is presented by the Muslims, observes that and is safely.

So these are some of the issues and rule and regulations that are affiliated with the end of this month. And I ask Allāh All Noble the Lord of the Great Throne to

[59]

end this month of us all together, the month of Ramadhan with pardon, forgiveness, and savior for the Hell-Fire. I ask Him Sublime and High in His Majesty, to bring us again to reach the month of Ramadhan in many years and time to come, and we are in obedience (to Allāh), having faith, good health, peace and Islam. And I ask Him Sublime and High in His Majesty, to set us right in our religion which is a safeguard of our affairs and set right for us our worldly life which is our way of living, and set right for us our life of the Hereafter which is our eternal destiny depends upon, and make our life for us a source of abundance and make our death a source of comfort for us protecting us for all evil and to forgive us and our Scholars and our parents and the Muslim men and women, those who are alive and those who have passed away. O Allāh forgive us of the earlier and the later open and our secret (sins) and our open (sins) and You know us better than our own selves, You are the First and the Last. There is no true God except You. O Allāh forgive us of all our sins, small and big and first and last, secret and open. O Our Lord, indeed we have oppressed ourselves, and if You do not forgive us then surely we are amongst the losers. O Our Lord give us good in this life and the Hereafter and save us from the torment of the Hell-Fire. O Allāh, aid us and not

[60]

against us, help us and not against us, plan for us and do not plan against us, and guide us and make guidance accepted by us with ease, and help us against those who oppress us, O Allāh make us from those who constantly mention You, and those who are thankful, and returning to You, and submitting to You, and obedient. O Allāh accept our repentance, and purify us of our sins, and make our evidence firm, and guide our hearts to and straighten our tongues and remove hatred from our hearts. O Allāh indeed we ask You for all the good in this life and the Hereafter, that which is known to us an unknown and we seek refuge with You from all evils in this life and the Hereafter. O Allāh indeed we ask You for the good that Your Slave and Messenger Muhammad (ﷺ) asked for, and we seek refuge with You from the evil that Your Slave and Messenger Muhammad (ﷺ) sought refuge with You from it. O Allāh indeed we ask You to grant us Paradise and that which brings us close to it from righteous statements and deed and we seek refuge with You from the Hell-Fire and that which brings us close to it from evil statements and deeds. O Allāh grant to our souls sense of righteousness and piety and purify them, as You are the Best Purifier of them. And You are the Protector and Guardian of them. O Allāh indeed we ask you for right guidance and safeguard

[61]

against evils, and chastity and richness from want. O Allāh unto You we have surrendered and unto You we affirm our faith, and to You we have reposed our trust and unto You we have repented and with You we seek help against our adversaries. We seek refuge in You from Your Might; there is no true God except You, Lead us not astray as You are Ever-Living, no death and the mankind and Jinn they die. O Allāh, Who controls the hearts, make our hearts firm upon obedience to You. O Allāh resurrect us as Muslims and cause us to die as believers, and join us with the righteous ones without disgrace and infatuation. O Allāh beautify us with faith and guidance of those rightly guided. O Allāh indeed we ask You for the irresistible sight of staring at Your Face and desire of meeting You without sadness and harm and being infatuated with misguidance. O Allāh split for us from fearing You that will save us from Your disobedience, and from Your obedience that will grant us Your Paradise, and certainty that will lighten for us the catastrophes of this worldly life. O Allāh grant us enjoyment of our hearing and vision and our strength as long as You have given us life and make them a good inheritance for us and take revenge on who oppressed us and help us against our enemy and do not make our catastrophe for us in our religion and do not make this worldly life our main focus and not our level of knowledge and do not impose upon us who will not have mercy upon us. O Allāh aid our weak Muslim brothers everywhere. O Allāh aid them who are in Damascus and Burma and everywhere. O Allāh aid them with greatest of support O Ever-Living O Everlasting. O Allāh preserve them with that You preserve Your righteous servants. O Allāh protect them from the front, behind, on their right, and on their left O Owner of Majesty and Honor. O Allāh give them safety in their fears, and shelter them and spare their blood O Ever-Living O Everlasting. O Allāh destroy Your enemy and their enemy. O Allāh choke them, and we seek refuge with You from their evils. O Allāh whoever wants evil for us or for any one of our Muslim brothers anywhere, then busy himself and make his plot turn on him, and make his plotting be his destruction O Ever-Living O Everlasting O! Owner of Majesty and Honor. O Allāh give us safety in our homelands and set right our Muslim Leaders and those in charge of our affairs and place in charge of our affairs of who fears You and is aware of You and follows what pleases You O Lord of All the Worlds. O Allāh give success to our Muslim Leader and Your guidance and aid him upon Your obedience O Ever-Living O Everlasting and provide him with righteous,

[63]

THIRD: RULES AND REGULATIONS
DEALING WITH THE EID PRAYER

advisable company O Lord of all the Worlds. O Allāh grant him enjoyment of good health and well-being and give him success in all that is pleasant. O Allāh give success to all the Muslim Leaders are living upon Your Book (Quraan) and judging according to Your Legislation and following the Sunnah of Your Prophet Muhammad (ﷺ). O Our Lord grant us with good in this worldly life and in the Hereafter with good and save us from the torment of the Hell-Fire, and our last supplication is All praise is due to Allāh the Lord of All the Worlds.

And may the blessings and favors of Allāh be upon His Slave and Messenger Muhammad and his wives and his companions altogether.

Coming soon…

Points of Benefit

Page:	Benefit:

Points of Benefit

Page:	Benefit:

Points of Benefit

Page:	Benefit: